TAKE A STAND

MY HERO JOURNAL

THIS BOOK BELONGS TO:

....

Caroline Rowlands

C

CARLTON
BOOKS

TIME TO TAKE A STAND

What's in this book?

This book is all about YOU, but it's also about some of the bravest, boldest and greatest HEROES of our time. Fill this journal with all the things that matter to YOU, discover your hopes and DREAMS and make plans for your FUTURE with the help of inspirational HEROIC legends, from NELSON MANDELA and GALILEO to QUEEN ELIZABETH I and JK ROWLING. Learn about the kind of person you are now... and the person you want to be.

THERE ARE LOTS OF JOURNAL PAGES FOR YOU TO WRITE, DRAW AND STICK PHOTOS IN.

DREAMING OF...

Fill this page with all your hopes and dreams.

My dream...

JOB
HOME
HOLIDAY
OUTFIT
MEAL

List three things you dream of achieving in the next...

YEAR

5 YEARS

What do you dream most about?

- school
- friends
- scary things
- family
- the future
- the past

WHAT DO YOUR DREAMS MEAN?

FALLING DREAMS dreaming you are falling from the sky or off a cliff can mean you feel out of control about something in your life.

FLYING DREAMS when you dream you are flying it can mean you're feeling confident about something in your life or you've had a recent success.

BEING NAKED DREAMS if you've ever dreamt you've forgotten to put your clothes on, it usually means you're a bit worried about something or can also mean you're trying to hide your true self.

WHAT WOULD A HERO DO?

After crash landing in the Amazon Rainforest and managing to find her way out of it, Juliane Koepcke always trusts her instincts and follows her dreams.

Q You dream of joining the Scouts, but your mates say it's a waste of time. What's the point in camping and hiking and caving and abseiling? Why do you need to learn how to tie a gazillion knots? Why can't you play video games like a normal person? What might Juliane Koepcke do?

A After surviving everything that the Amazon Rainforest threw at her, it's highly likely that Juliane would tell you to go for it. Scouting is about way more than tying knots. Just ask any of the millions of Scouts around the world.

JULIANE KOEPCKE

CHECK OUT ALL THE PAGES WITH FASCINATING FACTS ABOUT AMAZING HEROIC LEGENDS – SOME YOU'LL KNOW ALREADY AND SOME YOU MIGHT NOT.

FEEL INSPIRED WITH SOME MOTIVATIONAL TIPS, IDEAS AND QUIZZES TO BRING OUT YOUR INNER HERO.

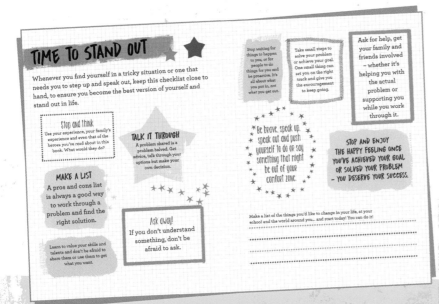

WITH INSPIRATIONAL FIGURES, HEROIC DEEDS AND LOTS OF IDEAS INSIDE, GET READY TO TAKE A STAND FOR WHAT YOU BELIEVE IN.

WHAT MAKES ME... ME!

There are about 7 billion people in the world and each and every one of them is different. So what makes you unique?

NAME
_____

AKA (also known as/nickname)
_____

AGE
_____

ADDRESS
_____

HEIGHT
_____

EYE COLOUR   HAIR COLOUR
_____

STRENGTHS/TALENTS
_____

DRAW OR STICK
A PICTURE OF
YOURSELF HERE.

I am always

(tick the ones that apply to you):

LAID BACK RELAXED CALM

BRAVE A GOOD LISTENER

A GOOD TALKER

HAPPY HARDWORKING

SHY AMBITIOUS EXCITABLE

I am sometimes

(tick the ones that apply to you):

A BIT OF A DREAMER SHY

KIND A BIT OF A JOKER

FUNNY

HELPFUL MYSTERIOUS

ADVENTUROUS HEROIC

BOLD CHILLED-OUT

Use the space below to write about something that really matters to you. It could be your friends, family, doing well at school or a cause you believe in.

_____

_____

_____

_____

_____

_____

_____

_____

_____

_____

_____

_____

_____

FRIENDS WITH...

Life is a lot more fun when you're with your friends. Make sure you surround yourself with the best people possible and those who will help you be the best person you can be too.

BEST FRIEND

OLDEST FRIENDS

OTHER FRIENDS

DOODLE A PICTURE OF YOU AND YOUR FRIENDS HERE.

Which friend would you choose to be by your side for these activities?

GOING TO A MOVIE
_____

GOING SHOPPING
_____

DOING HOMEWORK
_____

PLAYING SPORT
_____

EATING PIZZA
_____

WHAT WOULD A HERO DO?

ABRAHAM LINCOLN

Heroic ex-US President Abraham Lincoln wasn't just a great leader but a great friend to all kinds of people, from all sorts of backgrounds in the USA. He considered all people equal and went out of his way to help those less fortunate than himself and be kind to everyone, even his enemies.

Q A so-called best friend did something unforgiveable. (It's too unforgiveable even to write.) They've apologised, but you can't forget what they did. You don't think you'll EVER be able to treat them in the same way again. What would Abe do?

A Even after the horrors of the American Civil War, when asked by a General how to deal with the losing side, Abraham Lincoln told him to go easy. So maybe you can find it in your heart to give your friend a second chance.

'WHATEVER YOU ARE, BE A GOOD ONE.'

STANDOUT FRIENDSHIP QUALITIES

It goes without saying that you're always a good friend, or at least try to be. But what about the people you are friends with... what kind of people are they?

WHAT QUALITIES DO YOU LOOK FOR IN A FRIEND?

- ☐ loyalty
- ☐ kindness
- ☐ sense of humour
- ☐ brave
- ☐ generous
- ☐ outgoing
- ☐ forgiving
- ☐ heroic
- ☐ chilled out

What qualities do you avoid in a friend?

- ☐ selfishness
- ☐ a temper
- ☐ too chatty
- ☐ too quiet
- ☐ moody
- ☐ highly strung

DOODLE A PICTURE OF YOU AND YOUR FRIENDS HERE

Kindness and goodness rule when it comes to friendship and form the very foundation a good friendship is built on. Read on to discover some cool facts about some heroic figures who were both kind and good.

WHO?

Mary Seacole

WHEN?

Born 1805

WHAT MADE HER SUCH A GOOD PERSON?

Mary loved to help others, even strangers. She worked as a nurse in the Crimean War, saving many lives while risking her own.

Use this space to write about one of your friends and what makes them such a special friend and good person.

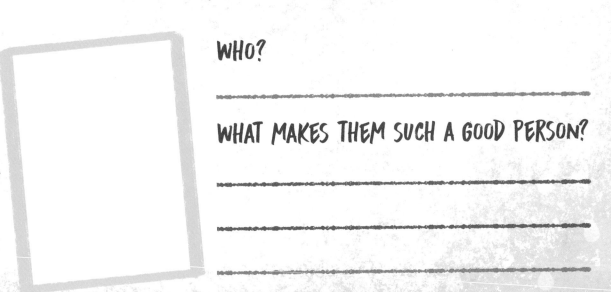

WHO?

WHAT MAKES THEM SUCH A GOOD PERSON?

ENJOYING...

What do you like to do in life? How do you fill
you time in between sleeping, eating and school?

I LOVE TO:

I ALSO LIKE TO:

I SOMETIMES ENJOY:

I HAVE ALWAYS WANTED TO:

Tick all the hobbies and activities you have tried and put
a star next to the ones you would like to try.

- SCOUTS/GUIDES
- NETBALL
- CYCLING
- SWIMMING
- CRICKET
- READING
- FOOTBALL

- RUNNING
- PLAYING MUSIC
- LISTENING TO MUSIC
- CRAFTING
- PAINTING
- DRAWING
- COOKING

- HORSE RIDING
- WATCHING MOVIES
- WATCHING TV
- SINGING
- KAYAKING
- CLIMBING
- HIKING

When it came to using her time wisely, Helen Keller certainly didn't hang about. Despite losing her hearing and sight when she was just two years old she went on to champion the rights of others and founded the Civil Liberties Union. The pie chart below shows how she spent her time. Create your own pie chart to show how you spend yours by following the simple steps below.

1. Make a shortlist of the five things you do most.

2. Then work out how much time you spend on these as a percentage.

3. Finally fill in the pie chart.

15% trying new things

5% giving lectures

10% writing

70% helping others

10% travelling

'THE ONLY THING WORSE THAN BEING BLIND IS HAVING SIGHT BUT NO VISION.'

HELEN KELLER

WHAT WOULD A HERO DO?

Q You're horribly, horribly shy. So when the school asks for volunteers to take part in a debating competition, you say no straight away – even though you'd dearly love to be involved. What would Helen Keller say?

A You know what's coming, right? Helen Keller would tell you to do it. Go for it. You're shy? No one will ever guess. Take a deep breath and give it a go. You might even enjoy it.

11

LEARNING ABOUT...

You spend, on average, 190 days a year at school – that's 1,235 hours a year! So make it count, be sure to appreciate your education and use it to take you to where you want to go in life.

NAME OF SCHOOL
....

BEST SUBJECT
....

FAVOURITE TEACHER
....

WORST TEACHER
....

MOST AMAZING THING YOU'VE LEARNED THIS YEAR

....

....

....

IF YOU WERE A TEACHER WHAT WOULD YOU TEACH AND WHY?

....

....

....

Tick your lunch option.
I eat...

- ☐ school dinners
- ☐ packed lunches

'However difficult life may seem, there is always something you can do and succeed at.'

Number these subjects from 1 to 9, with 1 for your favourite and 9 for your least favourite.

English ⚫	Languages ⚫
Maths ⚫	Science ⚫
Geography ⚫	Technology ⚫
History ⚫	Art ⚫
PE ⚫	

WHAT WOULD A HERO DO?

Professor Stephen Hawking was a maths, physicist and a cosmologist genius. In fact, he was pretty clever at most things and always top of his class at school.

STEPHEN HAWKING

Q Your homework makes no sense at all. Nada. Zero. Zilch. How on earth can you answer the questions if you don't understand them? And how can you tell your teacher that you don't understand them? It'll look as if you weren't paying attention in the lesson! What would Stephen Hawking say?

A Stephen Hawking wrote books so that people could understand complicated concepts. There's no way on earth – or in space – that he'd want you to be scratching your head. So pluck up the courage to go back and ask the teacher to explain it again. They won't mind. Just like Hawking, they want you to know more.

STANDOUT THINKERS

Even if you think what you learn at school isn't important, it most definitely is, as knowledge helps shape your mind and behaviour.

Galileo Galilei and Stephen Hawking were both geniuses and understood the importance of education and knowledge. They used their huge brains to make exciting and sometimes controversial discoveries, and weren't afraid to share them. They changed the way people thought and still think about the earth and universe forever.

The astronomer GALILEO GALILEI (born in 1564) realised that the Sun, not the Earth, was the centre of the universe. He had a choice. Should he ignore his findings, or should he speak out and risk upsetting the very powerful Catholic Church?

When the Church learned of his ideas, they made it illegal to support the theory. Initially Galileo kept quiet, but several years later he wrote a book which demonstrated that the theory was right.

The Catholic Church was furious. Galileo was called to Rome where he was questioned for a year (and nearly tortured) until he admitted he was wrong and that the Earth was stationary. Defiantly, he muttered 'yet it moves', so he spent the rest of his life under house arrest. It wasn't until 1992 that the Catholic Church finally admitted that Galileo was right!

GALILEO GALILEI

At the age of 21, STEPHEN HAWKING was diagnosed with ALS – a type of Motor Neurone Disease that affects the nerves that control movements like walking and talking. There was, and still is, no cure.

Doctors didn't expect him to live long. Although Hawking's speech worsened and he had to start using a wheelchair, he was determined to carry on with his life and his cosmology studies.

Hawking thought a lot about difficult subjects, including black holes, the Big Bang, general relativity, quantum theory, space-time and many other concepts. He even had a type of radiation named after him – Hawking radiation. When a computer company invented a speech-generating device that meant Hawking could communicate by moving his cheek, he could give lectures too.

He spoke and wrote about his discoveries in a way that everyone could understand. In A Brief History of Time (1988) he wrote about all the very latest ideas about the universe. The book was aimed at readers who knew nothing about cosmology. It was an instant bestseller, translated into over 30 languages and selling over 10 million copies worldwide.

STEPHEN HAWKING

THE NEXT TIME YOU LEARN SOMETHING INTERESTING, MAKE SURE YOU PASS IT ON AND SHARE YOUR NEW KNOWLEDGE WITH YOUR FAMILY AND FRIENDS.

TIME TO STAND OUT

Many people spend hours at the gym, running around a track or swimming lengths to help strengthen the muscles and organs in their bodies, but they often overlook the most important organ of all – the brain. Read on to discover how to make your brain the best it can be.

WHAT IS THE BRAIN?

Your brain is the command centre for your nervous system. It receives input from the sensory organs, like your eyes and ears, and sends output to your muscles. It is very complex and contains about 86 billion nerve cells and billons of nerve fibres.

REPEAT AFTER ME...

One of the best ways to help you remember things is repetition. So if you meet someone new and they say 'Hi, my name is Alice,' don't just say 'Hi', say, 'Hi Alice, nice to meet you!'

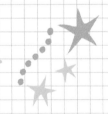

DO SOMETHING NEW

Every time you do something new, your brain wires new pathways to help you do this new thing. Then the more you repeat this new thing, the more pathways are created, enabling your brain to do lots of new things in lots of different ways. Learning a new language is one of the best ways to do this as it exposes your brain to a totally new way of thinking, so creates lots of new pathways, which will help your brain grow.

Why train your brain?

- it will help you learn things quicker

- it will help you remember things and stop you forgetting them, like people's names or birthdays

- to keep your brain healthy and working for longer

Concentrate

It's important you learn how to focus on the important things and avoid any distractions, that way all your efforts go into just one task and you achieve better results. So if you're doing your homework, make sure you switch off the TV, your phone etc. If you are tempted to give up on a hard task, push yourself to do just five minutes more of it. This will help you build up your mental stamina by pushing past the point of frustration.

LISTENING AND PLAYING...

Fill this page with all the different kinds of music you love to listen to and play.

Number these types of music from 1 to 9, with 1 for your most favourite and 9 for your least.

Jazz

Pop

Dance

Classical

Country

Hip Hop

R&B

Folk

Heavy Metal

Indie

Other

MY THREE FAVOURITE SINGERS ARE

1

2

3

MY THREE FAVOURITE SONGS ARE

1 _____

2 _____

3 _____

MY FAVOURITE BAND IS
_____

MY FAVOURITE SONG LYRICS ARE
_____

Colour in the musical instruments that you'd like to learn to play in green and the ones you wouldn't in blue.

LEADING OR FOLLOWING

It takes all kinds of people to make the world go round and there are those who lead and those who follow. But which are you?

I AM A...

⬤ LEADER   ⬤ FOLLOWER

WRITE AN EXAMPLE OF WHEN YOU'VE LED OR FOLLOWED WITH YOUR FAMILY OR FRIENDS

....

....

....

WRITE ABOUT ANY ACTIVITIES, LIKE SCOUTS, A SPORTS TEAM OR AT SCHOOL WHEN YOU HAVE SHOWN LEADERSHIP SKILLS

_____

_____

_____

USE THE SPACE BELOW TO WRITE ABOUT A GREAT LEADER THAT YOU ADMIRE, AND WHY. THEY COULD BE A FRIEND, SOMEONE YOU KNOW OR A HEROIC LEGEND, LIVING OR DECEASED

....

....

....

....

WHAT WOULD A HERO DO?

QUEEN ELIZABETH I

When Queen Elizabeth I was born in the sixteenth century, kings ruled. Everyone was nervous when Elizabeth took the throne. Who knew what would happen to the country if a woman was in charge? Would the new queen be able to stand up for herself and her country and lead a nation?

Q There's turmoil in the school football team. EVERYONE wants to be captain. You think you're good enough for the job, but how do you make everyone listen? How do you stand out, like Elizabeth I?

A Elizabeth I was smart. She would know that shouting and bawling was not the way to make everyone listen up. So she would calmly suggest that everyone put forward their plans for the captaincy. Maybe everyone should try out for the role? After all, it's a tough job. It's important to get the best person for the job.

STANDOUT LEADERS

The world has seen many heroic leaders who were not afraid to stand up and speak out for their beliefs.

QUEEN ELIZABETH I's reign lasted 45 years and it was a challenging one. Her sister, Mary, had brought back Catholicism during her rule. Elizabeth reversed this decision and reinstated the Church of England. Next there was a war with France to deal with. Plus, there was no shortage of people who wanted to take the throne from the queen.

Throughout her reign, Elizabeth had to stay strong to defeat her enemies. She even had Mary Queen of Scots, her own cousin, executed for treason. Elizabeth stepped up when her country needed her and her reign was later known as The Golden Age as she brought stability to her nation.

QUEEN ELIZABETH I

NELSON MANDELA was regularly arrested for speaking out his country's deeply unjust apartheid system. He was often put into jail for speaking out at rallies and finally imprisoned for 27 years – but he never gave up on his dream of ridding South Africa of apartheid. From behind bars he inspired others to keep protesting, and when FW de Klerk was elected as President, he set about banishing apartheid and freed Mandela.

Mandela and President de Klerk shared the Nobel Peace Prize in 1993. One year later, in an election where everyone, black or white, voted, Mandela became South Africa's first black president.

NELSON MANDELA

In 43 CE, the Romans invaded Britain. Of the many tribes they fought against, most were defeated at once and forced to obey their new rulers. But Prasutagus, king of the Iceni tribe, made a deal with the mighty Romans. If they allowed him to continue to rule alongside the invaders, his lands would be split between his offspring and the Romans when he died. Deal.

But when Prasatagus died in 60 CE, the Romans didn't keep their word and when Prasatagus' wife BOUDICCA protested about this, they beat her up and attacked her daughters. The Iceni queen was NOT happy. She wanted revenge. She rallied her people and some other Celtic tribes together to rebel against the Romans and led them all into battle. Boudicca's army destroyed Camulodonum (now known as Colchester), the capital of Roman Britain, then stormed on to Londinium (London). Boudicca was finally defeated, but became a legend for standing up to the Roman Empire and leading others to fight for what they believed in.

BOUDICCA

MARSHA P JOHNSON was a transgender icon and LGBTQ rights activist who helped those who suffered from prejudice and discrimination. She was born Malcolm Michaels Jr. But Johnson liked to dress as a girl. It wasn't until she left home and moved to New York, that she was able to live by her own rules. She gave herself a brand-new name – Marsha P Johnson. The P stood for 'Pay it no mind', because that's what she replied when anyone asked her if she was a man or a woman or gay or straight. What she meant was – ignore it – and this brave attitude inspired others and led them to be true to themselves too.

MARSHA P JOHNSON

WEARING...

Nothing helps you stand out from the crowd more than an individual sense of style. Write about your own fashion favourites on these pages.

TICK THE ITEMS YOU LOVE TO WEAR AND PUT A CROSS NEXT TO THE ONES YOU DON'T.

jeans ⬤   skirt ⬤   jacket ⬤   dress ⬤

trousers ⬤   jumper ⬤   leggings ⬤   t-shirt ⬤

shorts ⬤   shirt ⬤   hoody ⬤   blazer ⬤

MY FAVOURITE CELEBRITY STYLE ICON IS

BECAUSE

MY FAVOURITE FASHION BRAND OR SHOP IS

BECAUSE

DRAW YOUR FAVOURITE OUTFIT IN THE SPACE BELOW.

TICK YOUR FAVOURITE SHOPPING OPTION:

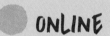 ONLINE  IN STORE

SHOP WITH CARE

- Take the time when you choose your clothes to think about where they come from, who is making them and what they are made from.

- Think about the effect your shopping choices have on the countries they are made in and the wider environment.

- Dress in a style you are comfortable in, so you'll not only look good but feel good too.

25

WATCHING...

Screen time doesn't necessarily have to be a waste of time, not when you get to watch all the tv shows and movies you love or discover things to inspire you.

My favourite TV show is

_____

My favourite movie is

_____

MY FAVOURITE ACTOR IS

_____

_____

_____

NAME SOME MOVIES THAT MADE YOU FEEL...

happy   sad   angry

HOW OFTEN DO YOU WATCH THE NEWS OR READ THE NEWS ONLINE OR IN PRINT?

daily   weekly   monthly

TICK THE KINDS OF MOVIES YOU LIKE TO WATCH AND CROSS THE ONES YOU DON'T.

comedy ⬤

action adventure ⬤

animation ⬤

mystery ⬤

sci-fi ⬤

costume drama ⬤

biography ⬤

western ⬤

fantasy ⬤

NAME A MOVIE THAT CHANGED THE WAY YOU THINK ABOUT SOMETHING IN LIFE, THEN WRITE WHY.

....

....

WHAT WOULD A HERO DO?

Irena Sendler was a social worker during World War II and bravely risked her life to help Jewish children escape being sent to concentration camps by the Nazis. By the end of the war she had heroically saved around 400 children.

Q You've seen some terrible stories on the news about children suffering in a war zone far away. You want to help, but you don't know how. How do you stand up, like Irena Sendler?

A If Irena Sendler wasn't old enough to go and help in person, she would probably have tried to help from home. She might begin by raising awareness, or she might raise money to help others help the children.

STANDOUT TALENT

Some writers, leaders and sporting heroes have achieved such amazing things that their lives or their creative work has been transformed for the big screen.

MUHAMMAD ALI was a legend inside the boxing ring... and outside it too. He achieved worldwide fame as a professional boxer. He had speed, stamina and skill. He was clever too – and funny. But when he stood up for his beliefs and refused to do his military service in the USA, he was banned from the sport for three years. His popularity plummeted but then people began to support his stance and admired him for speaking out about this and then civil rights issues.

He has featured in many documentaries about his life and in 2001 the actor Will Smith was nominated for an Oscar for his portrayal of Ali in the movie Ali.

'I am the part you won't recognise. But get used to me – black, confident, cocky; my name, not yours; my religion, not yours; my goals, my own. Get used to me.'

MUHAMMAD ALI

WHAT LEGEND-INSPIRED HERO MOVIES HAVE YOU SEEN?

If you could make a movie, who would you make it about and why?

JK ROWLING is one of the most famous authors of all time. Her seven Harry Potter® books have sold more than half a billion copies and been translated into 80 different languages. With such huge success, you'd expect Rowling to forget about her life before Harry. Except she hasn't, because she gives a lot of her money to charity and uses her celebrity to shine a spotlight on good causes. She is the president of Gingerbread – a UK charity working with single parent families. She founded Lumos – named after the light-giving spell in the Harry Potter® series – a charity that aims to help the millions of children in orphanages around the world find new homes. When Rowling feels strongly about something, she's not afraid to say (and tweet) exactly what she thinks. Whether it's politics, bigotry, homophobia, women's rights, religion, bullying or abuse, she won't stand for it and speaks out.

JK ROWLING

WORKING AT...

Do you ever look to the future and wonder what kind of job you'll end up doing? Or have you got your career path all mapped out?

NUMBER THE JOBS BELOW FROM 1 TO 10, WITH 1 FOR THE JOB YOU'D LIKE TO DO MOST AND 10 FOR THE ONE YOU'D LIKE TO DO LEAST.

teacher ⬤   banker ⬤   engineer ⬤

vet ⬤   chef ⬤   builder ⬤

doctor ⬤   journalist ⬤

astronaut ⬤   lawyer ⬤

ON AVERAGE, PEOPLE WORK FOR UP TO 35 YEARS OF THEIR LIVES AND ABOUT 8 HOURS A DAY. TICK THE THE PLACES YOU WOULD YOU LIKE TO WORK, AND CROSS THE ONES YOU WOULDN'T.

at home ⬤   in an office ⬤   in a forest ⬤

abroad ⬤   on a farm ⬤   on/in a vehicle ⬤

underwater ⬤   in space ⬤

DO YOU KNOW ANYONE WITH A REALLY INTERESTING OR INSPIRING JOB? WRITE ABOUT THEM, WHAT THEY DO AND WHY IT INSPIRES OR INTERESTS YOU BELOW.

_____

_____

_____

_____

WHAT WOULD A HERO DO?

Mary Seacole's father was a soldier and her mother was a nurse who taught Mary all her skills. Mary travelled all the way to the battle front of the Crimean War to help the wounded soldiers and overcame many obstacles to fulfil her dreams because she wanted to make a difference in other peoples' lives.

MARY SEACOLE

Q You're pretty sure that it doesn't take a rocket scientist to change a bike chain and you'd like to give it a go. But your dad doesn't think you can do it. He's threatening to take it to the bike repair shop instead. How do you stand up, like Mary Seacole?

A Mary Seacole wasn't a trained nurse, but she managed to learn. So first, try and persuade your dad. And if he still won't let you change the bike chain, go to the repair shop and watch it being done. Then you can work some mechanical magic next time.

TIME TO STAND OUT

It's easy to just exist in the world, but to make a difference you need to stand up and stand out for what you believe in. One way to do this is to get a stand-out career.

Take this quick quiz to work out how to make a start in getting the career you want:

1. The ultimate goal of your dream job is to:

A. Be in charge.
B. Make a difference in the world.
C. Be heard by millions of people.

2. Which is most true about you?

A. You like to have all the latest gadgets and technology.
B. You're more interested in other people than yourself.
C. You spend most of your time on your phone or computer.

3. If you could spend the next school holidays doing one thing, what would it be?

A. Campaigning for your local MP.
B. Volunteering at a local company.
C. Building up your following on Instagram and Twitter.

4. If you could choose, what are you most interested in doing:

A. Changing people's minds.
B. Making people's lives better.
C. Connecting with people.

ANSWERS:

MOSTLY A'S you should get an internship job to experience the kind of work you want to do first hand. Usually you have to work for free for several months but your travel and food expenses will be paid for and you'll get invaluable work experience in your chosen field.

MOSTLY B'S volunteer for a charity close to your heart and you'll find fulfilling work that will make a difference to your life and others. Check out https://do-it.org for some charities that might interest you.

MOSTLY C'S write a blog and start connecting with the world and sharing your views right now. Who knows where it might lead!

SOME HEROIC FIGURES WERE STAND-OUT STUDENTS...

Martin Luther King skipped school years because he was so clever, and became a doctor by the age of 25.

Stephen Hawking's parents were both academics and they all used to read books at the dinner table.

But some heroic figures had to do it the hard way – Abraham Lincoln didn't go to a fancy school or university. He grew up in a log cabin and was very poor. He had to work from a young age to support his family, but used books to educate himself.

Nelson Mandela managed to get to university but then got expelled for protesting. He didn't let that put him off achieving his dreams though.

Use this diagram to help you work out your dream job and visualise your future. Start by thinking about what you love, what pays well and what you're good at, then write them in the circles, then work out which might overlap to help you realise your dreams.

WHAT YOU LOVE

HAPPY BUT POOR

SKILLS NEEDED

WIN

WHAT YOU ARE GOOD AT

WHAT PAYS WELL

RICH BUT BORED

DRAWING...

You may not be able to draw much more than a stick man, or perhaps you have serious talent.

Whatever your skills, it's always good to look at the world around you and try and see it from a different perspective... and art is a great way to help you do this.

Does your home have many pictures on its walls? What kinds of pictures are they? Write about your favourite picture in the space below and describe why you like it so much:

....

....

....

Take a closer look at the things and people around you, as sometimes, when you look closer and think about what you are seeing, you can see things differently. Check out the picture to the right – what do you see? Now take a closer look... can you see something else? The answer is below.

Answer: There are two faces on either side of the tree!

USE THE SPACE BELOW TO DRAW A PICTURE THAT MEANS SOMETHING TO YOU. IT COULD BE A PERSON, A PLACE OR A MEMORY.

ONLINE

Fill in this page with everything you love about the online and digital world.

NUMBER THE MEDIA CHANNELS BELOW FROM 1 TO 5, WITH 1 FOR YOUR FAVOURITE AND 5 FOR YOUR LEAST FAVOURITE.

Facebook ○   Instagram ○   WhatsApp ○

Twitter ○   YouTube ○

TICK THE KINDS OF BLOGGERS, VLOGGERS, WEBSITES AND MEDIA CHANNELS YOU LIKE TO FOLLOW AND CROSS THE ONES YOU DON'T.

pranks ○   campaigning ○   political ○

news ○   fashion ○   sport ○

music ○   travel ○

IF YOU HAVE A YOUTUBE CHANNEL, VLOG OR BLOG, OR WOULD LIKE TO CREATE ONE, USE THE SPACE TO PLAN IT BELOW.

NAME OF YOUR CHANNEL/BLOG

....

THEME

....

POSTING FREQUENCY (tick one)

daily ⚪   weekly ⚪   monthly ⚪

COLLABORATORS (list who you'd like to work with online, eg friends or celebrities)

....

....

WHAT WOULD A HERO DO?

Online bullying can be a problem and it's important to shut out the negative voices online that will hurt you. JK Rowling is great at shutting down bullies online.

Q You're being bullied. You don't want to tell anyone, because you're worried that the bullies will find out and the bullying will get even worse. How do you stand up, like JK Rowling might do?

A Rowling was bullied at school, so she knows how awful it can be. Now, she blasts Twitter bullies with a witty comeback. It makes the rest of the world laugh and the bullies feel stupid. So prepare a few witty remarks to throw back next time!

READING...

To slightly misquote Dr Seuss, the more you read, the more you'll know; the more you know, the farther you'll go! Reading is a great way to broaden your mind, gain knowledge and find inspiration. Fill this page with everything you love about books.

WRITE THE NAMES OF THREE OF YOUR FAVOURITE AUTHORS BELOW.

_____

_____

_____

WRITE THE NAME OF YOUR FAVOURITE BOOK AND WHY.

_____

_____

_____

FILL IN THE BOOK SPINES WITH ALL THE BOOK
TITLES YOU'VE READ, OR WOULD LIKE TO READ.

DO YOU KEEP
A DIARY?

Yes ⬤   No ⬤

STAND OUT WRITERS

For some, the pen is mightier than the sword and words speak louder and say more than actions ever can. Read on to discover some heroic writers who helped to change the world.

Living in captivity in a small attic was not a pleasant experience for ANNE FRANK. But she knew it was important she and her family were never discovered by the Nazis, as they would be sent to a concentration camp or killed.

Her release valve was her diary. 'The nicest part is being able to write down all my thoughts and feelings; otherwise I'd absolutely suffocate,' she wrote. And when she heard that the Dutch government wanted people to keep diaries and documents to remember the occupation, she rewrote sections of her diary, in the hope that one day it would be published.

But on 4 August 1944, the Nazis stormed the annexe. Everyone inside was sent to concentration camps. By the following year, Anne was dead.

ANNE FRANK

Her father was the only one to survive and in 1947, just as Anne had wanted, he helped to get Anne's diary published. The Diary of a Young Girl by Anne Frank has been translated into over 70 languages, and read by millions around the world.

MAYA ANGELOU was a civil-rights activist, a poet, an author, a composer, an actress, a professor and a cable-car conductor... Her life was anything but easy, but that didn't stop her excelling at one thing after another. So perhaps the best way of describing her is as an all-singing, all-dancing superstar. (In fact, she was a singer and a dancer too!)

I Know Why the Caged Bird Sings tells the story of Angelou's troubled childhood and how she was affected by prejudice, racism, sexism and segregation. It tells how Angelou's employer changed her name from Marguerite to Mary, because it was easier to say. It tells how the Ku Klux Klan – a racist movement – terrorised her neighbourhood and how a white dentist refused to treat her because she was black.

MAYA ANGELOU

But the book also tells how she fought back, striking a chord with readers – both those who'd suffered from the same issues as Angelou and those who had no idea such unacceptable things happened. It was an instant hit and nominated for the National Book Award.

What authors inspire you? Have you ever read something that changed the way you think about history or your life? Write about it in the space below.

· ·

· ·

FAMILY MATTERS...

Your family love you, support you and are always there for you – fill this page with who's who you in your family.

LIST OUT YOUR FAMILY BELOW AND DRAW OR STICK IN A PICTURE OF THEM.

NAME
_____

RELATIONSHIP TO YOU
_____

BEST THING ABOUT THEM
_____

NAME
_____

RELATIONSHIP TO YOU
_____

BEST THING ABOUT THEM
_____

NAME
_____

RELATIONSHIP TO YOU
_____

BEST THING ABOUT THEM
_____

NAME
_____

RELATIONSHIP TO YOU
_____

BEST THING ABOUT THEM
_____

NAME
_____

RELATIONSHIP TO YOU
_____

BEST THING ABOUT THEM
_____

WHAT WOULD A HERO DO?

Family history can be fascinating and your family's past experiences can help shape your future ones, so make sure you talk to your family and listen to what they're saying.

Q You've quizzed the oldest members of your family and it turns out that there are some seriously cool stories just waiting to be told. But how? What would Maya Angelou do?

A Angelou was never trapped by a single medium – she used all of them. So she'd consider transforming a family history into a biography, poetry, a school play, a song or modern dance. Or maybe she'd use a whizzy app to make a movie about it – and then star in it too. And whatever you choose, just go for it. Maya Angelou would.

MAYA ANGELOU

43

REMEMBERING...

Keep your important memories alive by recording them here.

My best memories...

My worst memories...

Can you (or your parents) remember how old you were when you...

- CRAWLED FOR THE FIRST TIME
- WALKED FOR THE FIRST TIME
- TALKED FOR THE FIRST TIME
- GOT YOUR FIRST TOOTH
- LEARNED TO SWIM

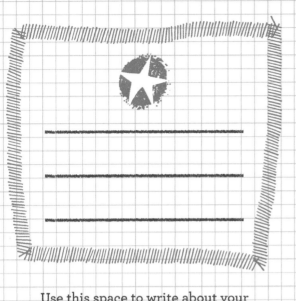

Use this space to write about your achievements and significant moments. This could be anything from a Scouts' badge, to passing a music exam, to learning to make your own breakfast.

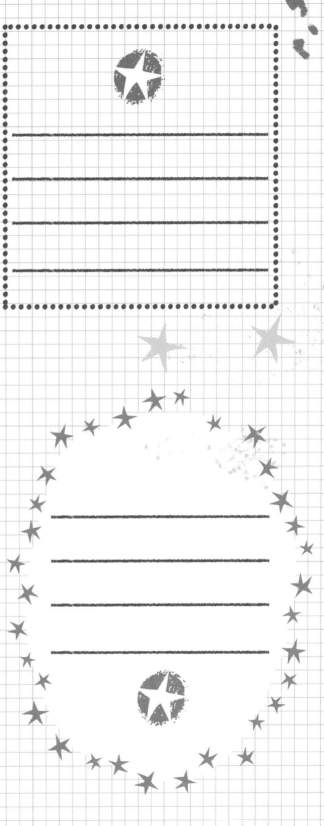

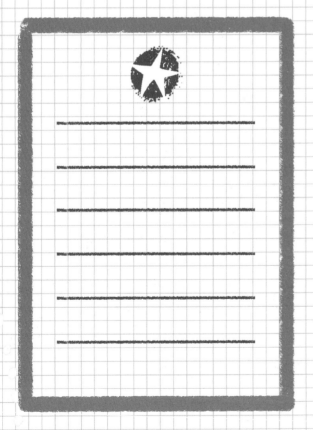

STANDOUT GAME CHANGERS

Some people aren't content to sit by when they see an injustice. They stand up and speak out about it. It doesn't matter if they're a president or a slave, a queen or a teenager, they are determined to do something and make a difference.

Around 100 BC, a Gladiator called SPARTACUS led a rebellion against his Roman captors. Fed up of being forced to fight for the Roman's entertainment and live as a slave, Spartacus escaped and led a number of his fellow slaves to Mount Vesuvius. The Romans sent soldiers to fight this rebellion and for over a year the two sides battled.

Spartacus was most probably killed in battle, but in the Hollywood re-telling of his story, the movie ends with the Romans telling the defeated slaves that their lives will be saved if they will identify their leader. Before Spartacus can speak, one by one all of his slave army stand up and cry out 'I am Spartacus', willing to stand by their brave leader and die for him.

SPARTACUS

MARTIN LUTHER KING JR dreamed that all people would be equal and was determined to put an end to segregation in the USA. He led a boycott of buses to force a change in the law that black people had to sit in just one part of the bus. It was a peaceful protest, but even so, King Jr was arrested and his home was bombed.

Still, the protestors kept going and at last – after 381 days – the US Supreme Court ruled against Montgomery's segregation law. The civil-rights protestors had won and King Jr continued raising awareness about the struggle for equality.

In 1963, King Jr gave his famous 'I Have a Dream' speech and inspired a nation The Civil Rights Act of 1964 banned discrimination against people based on their race, colour, religion or national origin. The same year, King Jr was awarded the Nobel Peace Prize but tragically, four years later, he was killed.

MARTIN LUTHER KING JR

KATHRINE SWITZER wanted to run the Boston Marathon, but in the 1960s, women weren't allowed to take part. On her registration, Switzer used her initials instead of her first name, so no one knew that she was a woman.

Wearing the number 261, Switzer set off. But she'd barely run 3km when a furious race official grabbed her and tried to pull her off the course. Switzer was terrified. But she got away and kept going — completing the marathon in a time of 4 hours 20 minutes. She'd done it!

After the race, Switzer campaigned so that women could officially enter the Boston Marathon. Thanks in part to her efforts, the 1984 Olympic Games included a women's marathon, helping to change public opinion of women runners.

KATHRINE SWITZER

TIME TO STAND OUT

Procrastination (which is when you put off doing something) happens when your dreams and goals are bigger than your energy levels, the time you have and sometimes your courage.

But next time you have a problem or see something you want to change, read on for how to do it.

STEP BY STEP

1. First up, approach the problem with a **POSITIVE MENTAL ATTITUDE.** Think about the things you are grateful for and glad you have in your life, rather than all the things you don't have.

2. Next, **VISUALISE** how you might feel the day after you've solved your problem or changed something.

3. Then identify **ONE SMALL THING** you can do today or this week to move towards your goal. Once this is done, you'll have made a start and feel a lot better.

4. Surround yourself with a **SUPPORT TEAM** to help you work through your problem. They can offer advice when needed or just be your cheering squad to keep you going when you feel like giving up.

5. **EXPECT FAILURE**... you can't always succeed in life and if you're prepared for the shock of not achieving your goals, you'll be better prepared to deal with it and pick yourself up and try again.

HOW TO CHANGE THE WORLD

1. **PAY IT FORWARD.** A small act of kindness, from just smiling at someone, to doing a siblings' chore can create a ripple effect. Small acts of kindness will also make you feel better, so it's a win-win!

2. **GROW THINGS.** Even a small patch of flowers or vegetables in your garden or on your windowsill will encourage and support wildlife.

3. Find out more about **WHAT YOU BUY** and where it comes from. Make considered choices as to what you need and where you shop. Pay attention to labelling on the products in your life and do some research into the brands you are loyal to – do they deserve your loyalty?

4. **VOLUNTEER!** From helping a neighbour to wash their car or collect their groceries to walking dogs for an animal shelter, there are people out there that need your help, right now.

HOW TO CHANGE A LAW

If you feel strongly about a law in your country, then do something about it. Rally your friends, family, teachers... and create a petition that asks for a change to the law or to government policy. Get 10,000 signatures and your petition will get a response from the UK government. Get 100,000 signatures and your petition will be considered for debate in Parliament.

PLAYING...

Fill in this page with all the things you love about playing and watching sport.

NUMBER THESE SPORTS FROM 1 TO 10, WITH 1 FOR YOUR FAVOURITE AND 10 FOR YOUR LEAST, EITHER TO WATCH OR PLAY.

- FOOTBALL
- RUGBY
- CRICKET
- SWIMMING

- NETBALL
- HOCKEY
- BASEBALL
- ATHLETICS

- BASKETBALL
- SKIING
- OTHER
- _____

	In school	Out of school
Monday		
Tuesday		
Wednesday		
Thursday		
Friday		
Saturday		
Sunday		

Write down any teams you play for, and what position.

TEAM NAME   **POSITION**

LIST YOUR TOP THREE SPORTING HEROES

_____

_____

_____

WRITE DOWN THREE SPORTS THAT YOU'D LIKE TO TRY

_____

_____

_____

WHAT WOULD A HERO DO?

Nelson Mandela never took no for an answer. He stayed strong and continued to fight for what he wanted, even when times got really tough, and he never let anyone put him off.

Q You're so excited. You've been practising basketball non-stop and you'd love to try out for the school team. But the coach isn't interested. 'I've already got the best team,' he says. 'There's no way you're good enough.' How do you stand up, like Mandela?

A Ahem. There's no need to be exactly like Mandela, of course and go to prison for your beliefs, but if you think something is unfair, then don't give up. Ask to go along to training sessions even if you don't get picked for the games, to help improve your game. Offer help out with carrying kit for games to show your commitment, and the coach might just give you a trial.

NELSON MANDELA

STANDOUT SPORTING HEROES

MUHAMMAD ALI was the first fighter to win the world heavyweight championship on three separate occasions; he successfully defended this title 19 times. After his retirement, Ali announced that he had Parkinson's disease, which affected his movement and speech. But he carried on making public appearances, using his legendary status to support charities and good causes. He was named a United Nations Messenger of Peace. He was also awarded the Presidential Medal of Freedom. In 1996, he was chosen to light the Olympic flame in Atlanta, USA.

MUHAMMAD ALI

KATHRINE SWITZER

KATHRINE SWITZER became the first woman to officially run the Boston Marathon in 1967, opening the door for other female runners to believe they could run in marathons all around the world. (Read more about her on page 47!)

JESSE OWENS

JESSE OWENS truly changed the world's perspective by challenging prejudices about race when he won four gold medals in the 1936 Summer Olympics of Berlin, in Nazi Germany. This was a powerful punch against Hitler's claims of the greatness of so-called 'pure Aryan blood'. Owens received the Presidential Medal of Freedom in 1976. In 1990, ten years after his death, he was also awarded the Congressional Gold Medal.

NANCY LIEBERMAN

When NANCY LIEBERMAN was hired as the head coach of the Dallas Mavericks' D-League affiliate, the Texas Legends, in 2009, she not only became the first woman head coach of men's pro basketball team, but became the first woman to coach a men's pro team in any sport.

A FEW OF MY FAVOURITE THINGS...

When you've had a tough day or just want to feel happy, surround yourself with all your favourite things and the world will seem a brighter place.

MY FAVOURITE...

friend

_____

FAMILY MEMBER

....

MOVIE

....

SONG

_____

TV show

_____

VLOGGER

....

CHOCOLATE BAR

....

shop

_____

animal

SPORT

FOOD

drink

time of year

DAY OF THE WEEK

EMOJI

DRAW YOUR MOST
FAVOURITE THING
OF ALL HERE:

DREAMING OF...

Fill this page with all your hopes and dreams.

My dream...

JOB

HOME

HOLIDAY

OUTFIT

MEAL

List three things you dream of achieving in the next...

YEAR

5 YEARS

What do you dream most about?

- ⬤ school
- ⬤ friends
- ⬤ scary things
- ⬤ family
- ⬤ the future
- ⬤ the past

WHAT DO YOUR DREAMS MEAN?

FALLING DREAMS Dreaming you are falling from the sky or off a cliff can mean you feel out of control about something in your life.

FLYING DREAMS When you dream you are flying it can mean you're feeling confident about something in your life or you've had a recent success.

BEING NAKED DREAMS If you've ever dreamt you've forgotten to put your clothes on, it usually means you're a bit worried about something, or it can also mean you're trying to hide your true self.

WHAT WOULD A HERO DO?

After crash landing in the Amazon Rainforest and managing to find her way out of it, Juliane Koepcke always trusts her instincts and follows her dreams.

Q You dream of joining the Scouts, but your mates say it's a waste of time. What's the point in camping and hiking and caving and abseiling? Why do you need to learn how to tie a gazillion knots? Why can't you play video games like a normal person? What might Juliane Koepcke do?

A After surviving everything that the Amazon Rainforest threw at her, it's highly likely that Juliane would tell you to go for it. Scouting is about way more than tying knots. Just ask any of the millions of Scouts around the world.

JULIANE KOEPCKE

Use this page to write about all the things you believe in or support.

If you could vote, which political party would you vote for and why?

_____

_____

_____

_____

IF YOU HAVE A FAITH, WRITE ABOUT YOUR RELIGION AND WHY IT'S IMPORTANT TO YOU.

....

....

....

....

TICK THE MORAL VALUES BELOW THAT YOU TRY TO LIVE BY

- say only nice things
- tell the truth
- have courage
- keep promises
- don't cheat

- treat everyone equally
- do not judge
- have patience
- be trustworthy

- be loyal
- show respect for others
- seek justice

DRAW OR STICK A PICTURE OF SOMEONE (PAST OR PRESENT) WHO YOU ADMIRE AND WRITE ABOUT WHY YOU ADMIRE THEM SO MUCH.

STANDOUT BELIEVERS

Whether it's spiritual, political or religious, some of the world bravest heroes were willing to risk their lives and freedom to stand up for what they believed in. Can you read these inspiring quotes and work out who said what?

(Answers at the bottom of the next page.)

1. If I quit everyone's going to believe a woman can't do this.

2. How many years has it taken people to realise that we are all brothers and sisters and human beings in the human race?

3. FLOAT LIKE A BUTTERFLY, STING LIKE A BEE.

4. I've reached a point in life where it's no longer necessary to try to impress. If they like me the way I am, that's good. If they don't, that's too bad.

5. The only thing worse than being blind is having sight but no vision.

6. Non-violence is the greatest force at the disposal of mankind. It is mightier than the mightiest weapon of destruction.

7. Freedom is never voluntarily given by the oppressor; it must be demanded by the oppressed.

8. If you don't like something, change it. If you can't change it, change your attitude.

Kathrine Switzer

Helen Keller

Marsha Johnson

Mahatma Ghandi

Muhammad Ali

Martin Luther King

Cory Aquino

Maya Angelou

TRAVELLING TO...

Do you dream of travelling the world or are you someone who believes there's no place like home? Fill this page with your holiday memories and travelling dreams.

MY BEST HOLIDAY MEMORY EVER:

MY WORST HOLIDAY MEMORY EVER:

PUT A TICK NEXT TO THE TYPES OF HOLIDAYS YOU LIKE AND A CROSS NEXT TO THE ONES YOU DON'T:

- camping
- safari
- sightseeing
- skiing
- beach
- activity
- diving

WHAT'S YOUR FAVOURITE WAY TO TRAVEL?

- on an aeroplane
- walking
- by hot-air balloon
- by boat
- by car

IF I COULD GO ON HOLIDAY WITH ANYONE I WOULD GO WITH:

_____

MARK THE CONTINENTS YOU'VE VISITED WITH A TICK ON THE MAP. MARK THE ONES YOU'D LOVE TO GO TO WITH A HEART.

STANDOUT TRAVELLERS

For some, travelling is not a holiday but a chance to explore, experience adventure and change the way we view the world. For others, it can turn into a matter of survival.

Write something you know about each of these world-famous explorers in the space below. It could be when they lived, where they explored or the kinds of people they were.

CHRISTOPHER COLUMBUS

JAMES COOK

GERTRUDE BELL

AMELIA EARHART

FRANCIS DRAKE

NEIL ARMSTRONG

SIR EDMUND HILARY

MARCO POLO

JULIANE KOEPCKE

When she was only 17 years old, JULIANE KOEPCKE was travelling by air when the plane flew into a thunderstorm. A lightning bolt hit a fuel tank, which exploded, ripping off one wing.

The plane crashed... but Koepcke didn't crash with it. Somehow, she was separated from the aircraft and, still strapped into her seat, she plummetedfrom the sky and unbelievably, she survived!

But she crash landed in the Amazon Rainforest and was all on her own. Her survival instincts kicked in and she set off to find a stream so that she'd have water to drink. She hoped that if she followed the water, it would lead to a river and hopefully civilisation – as long as she could avoid the caimans, piranhas, snakes and poisonous frogs on the way.

Koepcke followed the stream through the rainforest. She'd lost her glasses in the crash so it was difficult to see where she was going. She knew that many plants in the jungle were poisonous, so she didn't dare eat any of them. After a few days she was sunburnt, weak and very, very hungry. Then she saw a boat, and shelter too. But still there were no people. So she slept. The following evening, after 11 days in the rainforest, she was found by three forestry workers. She'd done it! She hadn't given up and had survived.

JANUARY

MY HIGHLIGHT OF THE MONTH

BIRTHDAYS TO REMEMBER

1	2	3	4	5	6	7
8	9	10	11	12	13	14
15	16	17	18	19	20	21
22	23	24	25	26	27	28
29	30	31				

ON THIS DAY IN HISTORY

JANUARY 15 1559 Elizabeth Tudor, daughter of Henry VIII and Anne Boleyn, was crowned as Elizabeth I in Westminster Abbey.

NOTES

FEBRUARY

SOMETHING I LEARNT THIS MONTH

BIRTHDAYS TO REMEMBER

1	2	3	4	5	6	7
8	9	10	11	12	13	14
15	16	17	18	19	20	21
22	23	24	25	26	27	28

ON THIS DAY IN HISTORY

15 FEBRUARY 1564 Galileo Galilei was born in Pisa, Italy.

NOTES

MARCH

BEST THINGS THAT HAPPENED THIS MONTH

BIRTHDAYS TO REMEMBER

1	2	3	4	5	6	7
8	9	10	11	12	13	14
15	16	17	18	19	20	21
22	23	24	25	26	27	28
29	30	31				

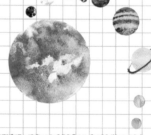

ON THIS DAY IN HISTORY
14 MARCH 2018 Stephen Hawking died.

NOTES

APRIL

MY HIGHLIGHT OF THE MONTH

BIRTHDAYS TO REMEMBER

1	2	3	4	5	6	7
8	9	10	11	12	13	14
15	16	17	18	19	20	21
22	23	24	25	26	27	28
29	30					

ON THIS DAY IN HISTORY

4 APRIL 1928 Maya Angelou was born St Louis, Missouri in the US.

NOTES

MAY

SOMETHING I LEARNT THIS MONTH

BIRTHDAYS TO REMEMBER

1	2	3	4	5	6	7
8	9	10	11	12	13	14
15	16	17	18	19	20	21
22	23	24	25	26	27	28
29	30	31				

ON THIS DAY IN HISTORY

10 MAY 1994 Nelson Mandela
became President of South Africa.

NOTES

JUNE

SOMETHING I LEARNT THIS MONTH

BIRTHDAYS TO REMEMBER

1	2	3	4	5	6	7
8	9	10	11	12	13	14
15	16	17	18	19	20	21
22	23	24	25	26	27	28
29	30					

ON THIS DAY IN HISTORY
12 JUNE 1929 Anne Frank was born in Frankfurt, Germany.

NOTES

JULY

BEST BITS ABOUT THIS MONTH

BIRTHDAYS TO REMEMBER

1	2	3	4	5	6	7
8	9	10	11	12	13	14
15	16	17	18	19	20	21
22	23	24	25	26	27	28
29	30	31				

ON THIS DAY IN HISTORY

6 JULY 1907 Frida Kahlo was born in Coyocoan, Mexico City, Mexico.

NOTES

AUGUST

PLANS FOR THIS MONTH

BIRTHDAYS TO REMEMBER

1	2	3	4	5	6	7
8	9	10	11	12	13	14
15	16	17	18	19	20	21
22	23	24	25	26	27	28
29	30	31				

ON THIS DAY IN HISTORY

13 AUGUST 1918 Opha May Johnson became the first woman to enlist in the United States Marine Corps.

NOTES

SEPTEMBER

BEST BITS ABOUT THIS MONTH
···

BIRTHDAYS TO REMEMBER
···

1	2	3	4	5	6	7
8	9	10	11	12	13	14
15	16	17	18	19	20	21
22	23	24	25	26	27	28
29	30					

ON THIS DAY IN HISTORY
10 SEPTEMBER 1982 Misty Copeland was born in Kansas City, Missouri, USA. Misty went on to become the first African American principal dancer for the American Ballet Theatre company.

NOTES
··
··

OCTOBER

MY HIGHLIGHT OF THE MONTH

....

BIRTHDAYS TO REMEMBER

....

1	2	3	4	5	6	7
8	9	10	11	12	13	14
15	16	17	18	19	20	21
22	23	24	25	26	27	28
29	30	31				

ON THIS DAY IN HISTORY

2 OCTOBER 1869 Mahatma Ghandi was born in Porbandar, India.

NOTES

NOVEMBER

SOMETHING I LEARNT THIS MONTH

BIRTHDAYS TO REMEMBER

1	2	3	4	5	6	7
8	9	10	11	12	13	14
15	16	17	18	19	20	21
22	23	24	25	26	27	28
29	30					

ON THIS DAY IN HISTORY

24 NOVEMBER 1859 Charles Darwin published 'On The Origin of Species' and changed humanity's view of its origins forever.

NOTES

DECEMBER

PLANS FOR THIS MONTH

BIRTHDAYS TO REMEMBER

1	2	3	4	5	6	7
8	9	10	11	12	13	14
15	16	17	18	19	20	21
22	23	24	25	26	27	28
29	30	31				

ON THIS DAY IN HISTORY

1 DECEMBER 1955 a bus driver asked a woman called Rosa Parks to give up her seat for a white man. She refused and set off a chain of events that resulted in civil rights laws in the USA being changed forever.

NOTES

TIME TO STAND OUT

Whenever you find yourself in a tricky situation or one that needs you to step up and speak out, keep this checklist close to hand, to ensure you become the best version of yourself and stand out in life.

Stop and think

Use your experience, your family's experience and even that of the heroes you've read about in this book. What would they do?

TALK IT THROUGH

A problem shared is a problem halved. Get advice, talk through your options but make your own decision.

MAKE A LIST

A pros and cons list is always a good way to work through a problem and find the right solution.

Ask away!

If you don't understand something, don't be afraid to ask.

Learn to value your skills and talents and don't be afraid to share them or use them to get what you want.

Stop waiting for things to happen to you, or for people to do things for you and be proactive. It's all about what you put in, not what you get out.

Take small steps to solve your problem or achieve your goal. One small thing can set you on the right track and give you the encouragement to keep going.

Ask for help, get your family and friends involved – whether it's helping you with the actual problem or supporting you while you work through it.

Be brave, speak up, speak out and push yourself to do or say something that might be out of your comfort zone.

STOP AND ENJOY THE HAPPY FEELING ONCE YOU'VE ACHIEVED YOUR GOAL OR SOLVED YOUR PROBLEM – YOU DESERVE YOUR SUCCESS.

Make a list of the things you'd like to change in your life, at your school and the world around you... and start today! You can do it!

LOOKING BACK...

Look back over your year and write the most important thing you've learnt and any changes that have happened in your life.

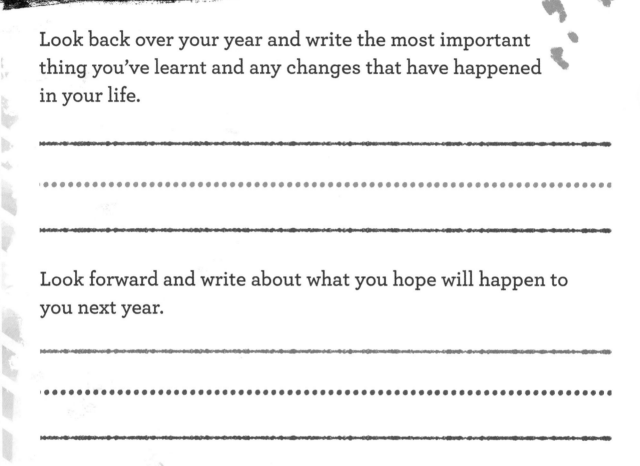

Look forward and write about what you hope will happen to you next year.

THIS IS A CARLTON BOOK

Published in 2019 by Carlton Books Limited, an imprint of the Carlton Publishing Group, 20 Mortimer Street, London W1T 3JW

Text and design copyright © Carlton Books Limited 2019

A catalogue record for this book is available from the British Library.

ISBN: 978 1 78312 465 7

Printed in Dongguan, China

10 9 8 7 6 5 4 3 2 1

Author: Caroline Rowlands

Executive Editor: Joff Brown
Art Editor: Deborah Vickers
Design: Rachel Lawston
Production: Nicola Davey

Illustrations and photographs by Anna Higgie, Anna Stiles, Jessica Singh, Jonny Wan, Kelly Thompson, Taylor Dolan, Sofia Bonatti, Margarida Esteves and Shutterstock